On Ladybug Farm, something is always cooking. Whether it's strawberry jam in the spring, blueberry scones in the summer, Brunswick stew in the autumn or Ida Mae's fruit cakes in the winter, the halls of the grand old mansion are always redolent of delicious flavors, and the kitchen is the heart of the home.

Based on her beloved Ladybug Farm series, the author of *A Year on Ladybug Farm*, *At Home on Ladybug Farm* and *Love Letters from Ladybug Farm* has put together this collection of most-requested recipes for her readers. Using fresh, seasonal ingredients with a dash of Southern flair, this collection is sure to be a favorite of amateur cooks both on and off Ladybug Farm.

A YEAR ON LADYBUG FARM
Three best friends discover an old house… and a new life.

AT HOME ON LADYBUG FARM
The old house begins to reveal its secrets, and the residents of Ladybug Farm learn what it means to be a family.

LOVE LETTERS FROM LADYBUG FARM
Wedding bells are ringing at Ladybug Farm, but what kinds of changes will they bring?

Praise for the Ladybug Farm series:

"Absolutely delectable"

--Publisher's Weekly

"A must read."

--Examiner.com

"A delight to read…"

--Book Binge

"If you are looking for a book to lift your spirits, this is it!"

--Library Thing.com

"Ball has crafted a page-turner"

--Georgia Mountain Laurel

Recipes From Ladybug Farm :

A Companion Cookbook

By Donna Ball

Recipes from Ladybug Farm

Table of Contents

Introduction

One of the first things readers always mention to me about the Ladybug Farm books is the food—how often it is described throughout the books, and how wonderful it all sounds. I'm often asked why food plays such an important part in the texture of the books, and for me the answer is simple: you can't write a book about women without also writing about food. Women are natural nurturers, and they do most of their nurturing—as well as their socializing—through food.

Don't expect this to be a traditional cookbook. I've organized it according to seasons, not logic, because when you eat what you grow—like Cici, Bridget and Lindsay learned to do—you make what you can out of what you have…and in the case of the ladies of Ladybug Farm, sometimes that's pretty spectacular. Like Ida Mae, I am an intuitive cook—a dash of this, a pinch of that—so feel free to experiment with these recipes and if you come up with something you like better, let me know.

Meantime, pull up a rocking chair on the front porch, pour yourself a glass of wine, and take your time browsing through the kitchen of Ladybug Farm. I hope you find something you love!

--*Donna Ball*

The Kitchen of Ladybug Farm

Bridget walked to the center of the enormous room, drew in a breath, and pressed both hands to her cheeks, turning full circle. "Oh, my goodness," she said.

The floor was paved in brick worn smooth by time, and the antique brick on the walls was oiled to a sheen. There was a raised cooking fireplace at one end of the enormous room where they could imagine placing a downy sofa and a couple of chairs for cozy winter evenings. The center island was soapstone, and the counter tops were tiled in cottage white and delft blue. The back splash behind the deep farmer's sink was a mural in the blue willow pattern. There were two big stoves, two dishwashers, a giant refrigerator and an upright freezer. "Obviously, the kitchen has been upgraded over the years, and the appliances are industrial grade," Maggie said. "The Blackwells did a lot of entertaining in their prime."

Bridget touched one of the stoves reverently. "Oh my God," she said. "This is a Viking."

"Bet you could whip up a casserole or two on that, huh Bridge?" said Lindsay with a grin.

"Of course all appliances are included," Maggie said. "And there's a butler's pantry."

Bridget dashed off to explore it, and in a moment they heard a muffled squeal of delight.

"I hate the tile," Cici said, but she was grinning too. It had been a long time since either of them had seen their friend this happy.

In a moment Bridget returned, breathless with excitement. "Unbelievable," she said. "The silverware drawers are lined with blue velvet. There's a pie safe with a lock! And just outside there's a walled herb garden. Some of the herbs are still growing. There's a rosemary bush as big as a tree!"

Maggie was looking very pleased with herself, and Cici knew what she was thinking, what any real estate agent worth her commission would think: the kitchen sells the house.

---A Year on Ladybug Farm

Recipes From Ladybug Farm

Strawberry Season

On Ladybug Farm, the best part of spring is strawberry season. The sunny hills are covered with vines, every basket, bowl and pot in the kitchen is filled with fruit, and for weeks at a time the entire house smells like strawberries, strawberries, strawberries.

Bridget's Strawberry Cobbler

- 1 cup flour
- 1 cup sugar
- 1 stick butter, softened
- 3 cups strawberries, hulled and sliced
- ¼ cup sugar
- 1 teaspoon vanilla extract
- 2 tablespoons cornstarch

Preheat oven to 350

Mix together flour, 1 cup sugar and butter in food processor or with a pastry cutter. In a separate bowl, toss strawberries with ¼ cup sugar, vanilla and cornstarch. Butter a deep 8 or 9 inch casserole dish and pour in strawberry mixture. Top with crumbled flour mixture, Place on baking sheet to catch spill-over, and bake until golden and bubbly, about 30 minutes.

Serve warm with whipped cream or vanilla ice cream.

Strawberry Trifle

- 1 angel food cake (store-bought is fine)
- 1 quart fresh strawberries, sliced
- 1 ½ cup sugar, divided
- 8 oz cream cheese, softened
- 8 oz. sour cream
- 1/4 cup plus 2 tablespoons amaretto, divided

Slice fresh strawberries and cover with 1 cup sugar. Add 2 tablespoons amaretto. Stir gently and let strawberries sit at room temperature until a syrup forms, about half an hour.

Tear angel food cake into cubes; set aside.

Mix sour cream, cream cheese and ½ cup sugar with 1/4 cup amaretto at medium speed on a mixer until smooth, about 3 minutes.

Line a trifle bowl (or any large, clear glass bowl) with 1/3 of the cubed angel food cake. Pour 1/3 of the strawberry mixture over it. Top with ½ the cream cheese mixture, spreading to edges as evenly as possible. Layer 1/3 of the cake cubes, top with 1/3 strawberry mixture. Spread remaining cream cheese on top. Top with remaining cake cubes, add remaining strawberry mixture. Cover and let sit overnight. Before serving, decorate with fresh sliced strawberries.

Ida Mae says...*Don't even bother with those cardboard strawberries you get from the store in the winter. Anything worth making is worth making fresh.*

Bridget says...*Sometimes I use strawberries frozen out of our garden.*

Strawberry Muffins

- 1/4 cup butter, melted
- 1/2 cup milk
- 1 egg
- 1/2 teaspoon salt
- 2 teaspoons baking powder
- 1/2 cup sugar
- 1 3/4 cups all-purpose flour
- 1 cup chopped strawberries

Preheat oven to 375 degrees.

In a small bowl, combine butter, sugar, milk, and egg. Beat lightly. In a large bowl, mix flour, salt, and baking powder together. Toss in chopped strawberries and stir to coat with flour. Pour in milk mixture and stir until well blended.

Fill 8 well-oiled muffin cups 2/3 full. Bake at 375 degrees F for 25 minutes, or until the tops bounce back from the touch. Cool 10 minutes and remove from pans.

Strawberry Pancakes

- 1 large egg
- 1 cup milk
- 1 teaspoon vanilla extract
- 2 tablespoons unsalted butter, melted, plus more for serving
- 1 cup strawberries
- 1-1/4 cups all-purpose flour
- 2 tablespoons granulated sugar
- 3 teaspoons baking powder
- 1/2 teaspoon salt
- Strawberry syrup, for serving (recipe follows)

In a blender or food processor, blend the wet ingredients together with the strawberries. Add the dry ingredients in thirds, blending after each addition.

Pour the batter onto a hot, well-buttered griddle 1/4 cup at a time. Turn when bubbles break on the top, 2-3 minutes. Cook until golden brown, about 2 minutes more. Serve with butter and strawberry syrup.

Strawberry Syrup:

- 1 cup strawberries, sliced
- ½ cup sugar
- 1 teaspoon lemon juice

Puree all ingredients together in a blender. Pour into small saucepan and bring to boil over low heat. Boil and stir for one minute. Strain through fine sieve or cheesecloth. Serve warm with pancakes.

Strawberry Shortcake

- 2 cups sliced strawberries
- ½ cup sugar

For cake:
- 1 cup white sugar
- 1/2 cup butter
- 2 eggs
- 2 teaspoons vanilla extract
- 1 1/2 cups all-purpose flour
- 2 teaspoons baking powder
- ½ cup milk

For topping:
- 1 cup heavy whipping cream
- ½ cup sugar
- 1 teaspoon vanilla extract

Preheat oven to 350. Grease and flour a 9 inch round pan

Mix strawberries and sugar together; set aside

In a medium bowl, cream together the sugar and butter. Beat in the eggs, one at a time, then stir in the vanilla. Combine flour and baking powder, add to the creamed mixture and mix well. Finally stir in the milk until batter is smooth. Pour or spoon batter into the prepared pan.

Bake for 30 to 40 minutes in the preheated oven, until cake springs back to the touch.Let cake cook for ten minutes, remove from pan.
 Cool completely.

(cont.)

Strawberry Shortcake *(cont)*

Meanwhile, whip cream until stiff peaks form, sprinkling in the sugar a tablespoon at a time. Stir in vanilla. Refrigerate.

Slice cake in half horizontally. Place one half on serving platter and spoon one half of the strawberries on top, allowing some of the juice to soak into the cake. Top with half the whipped cream. Add the other half of the cake, top with remaining strawberries and whipped cream.

Strawberry Coulis

- 6 cups strawberries, fresh or frozen
- 1 cup granulated sugar
- ¼ cup port wine or frambroise

Combine all the ingredients in a saucepan and bring the mix to a boil. Once it is boiling and the sugar has been dissolved, remove from heat and transfer the mixture to a blender.

Add wine or framboise and blend until it is very smooth, and then pass the sauce through a mesh strainer to remove the seeds. Serve as a topping for ice cream, cheesecake, or pound cake.

Creamy Strawberry Salad Dressing

- 1 cup fresh strawberries
- 1 clove garlic, minced
- 2 teaspoons honey
- Juice of one lemon
- ½ cup mayonnaise
- 1/4 teaspoon salt

Mix in blender until creamy. Store in tightly covered container in refrigerator for up to 3 days.

Bridget's Pan Bread

- ½ cup butter, very soft
- 2 cups flour
- 1 teaspoon soda
- ½ teaspoon salt
- 2/3 cup buttermilk
- 1 tablespoon chopped fresh rosemary
- ½ cup shredded cheddar cheese

Preheat oven to 425

Mix together flour, soda and salt in a bowl. Cut in butter with a pastry blender, fork or your fingers. Add buttermilk, rosemary and cheddar and blend with spoon just until mixed. Turn into a well-greased 8x8 skillet or cake pan and bake at 425 20-25 minutes. Serve warm with butter.

A Special Luncheon Menu

Minted Asparagus Soup

Four Cheese Soufflé with Roasted Pepper Puree

Mini Scones stuffed with Cherries and Cream Cheese

Wild Dandelion Salad with Raspberry Vinaigrette

Cheese Biscuits and Pinot Noir Jam

--Love Letters From Ladybug Farm

Minted Asparagus Soup

- 3 cups prepared chicken broth
- 2 bunches fresh asparagus, tender parts only
- juice of one lemon
- I cup chopped fresh mint
- 1 cup cream
- Salt to taste
- 3 slices smoked bacon, fried and crumbled
- Rosemary olive oil for garnish

Discard the woody ends of the asparagus and chop the green tender tips into one-inch pieces.

Bring chicken broth to a simmer and add asparagus; cook just until al dente, about 5 five minutes. Reserve one tablespoon chopped mint for garnish, and add the remainder to the asparagus. Stir in cream and continue cook just until warm (do not boil!), about 2 minutes. Remove from heat. Add lemon juice and transfer to blender (or use an immersion blender). Blend until smooth. Taste and salt if necessary.

Chill. Just before serving, top with a drizzle of rosemary-infused olive oil and a sprinkle or crumbled bacon .

Four Cheese Soufflé
with Roasted Red Pepper Puree

- ¼ cup butter
- ¼ cup   all-purpose flour
- 1 ¼ cup milk
- ¼ teaspoon cayenne
- ¼ teaspoon salt
- ½ cup shredded sharp cheddar cheese
- ½ cup pepper jack cheese
- ½ cup Gruyere cheese
- ½ cup Swiss cheese
- 6 large eggs, separated
- ¼ teaspoon cream of tartar

 Generously butter a 2-quart soufflé dish or six 1- to 1 1/4-cup soufflé dishes; if using small ones, set them about 2 inches apart in a 10- by 15-inch baking pan.

 In a 2- to 3-quart pan over medium heat, melt 1/4 cup butter. Add flour and stir until mixture is smooth and bubbly. Stir in milk, cayenne, and salt, stirring continuously until sauce boils and thickens, 3 to 4 minutes. Remove from heat.

Add cheese and stir until melted. Add egg yolks and stir until the mixture is blended and smooth.

 In a large bowl beat egg whites and cream of tartar on high speed until stiff peaks form. Fold a third of the cheese sauce into whites until well blended. Add remaining sauce and gently fold in just until blended.

Scrape the batter into the prepared soufflé dish . Bake in a 375° oven until top is golden to deep brown and cracks look fairly dry, 25 to 30 minutes for large soufflé, 15 to 20 minutes for small ones. Serve immediately on a bed of warm roasted red pepper puree.

Red Pepper Puree

2 large red bell peppers, roasted and chopped
¼ cup extra-virgin olive oil
1 ½ teaspoon fresh lemon juice
½ teaspoon salt

Place all ingredients in a blender and puree until smooth

Mini-Scones
Stuffed With Cherry Cream Cheese

* 2 cups flour
* ¼ cup sugar
* 3 teaspoons baking powder
* ½ teaspoon salt
* 8 tablespoons chilled butter, cut into pieces
* ½ cup dried cherries, chopped
* 1 egg
* ½ cup heavy cream
* 2 teaspoons almond flavoring
* Granulated sugar for sprinkling

Preheat oven to 350 and lightly grease a baking sheet.

Combine flour, sugar, baking powder, and salt. Work in the butter in small pieces using a pastry cutter or food processor until the mixture resembles pea-size crumbs.

Add dried cherries to flour mixture. Mix to coat.

In a small bowl, combine egg, heavy cream and almond extract. Whisk to combine. Add to flour mixture. Using a fork, combine to form large clumps.

Turn the dough out onto a lightly floured surface and knead 5-6 times. Roll into a 9 inch square , cut into 1inch circles with a cookie cutter, miniature biscuit cutter, or medium bottle cap.

Place on greased baking sheet and sprinkle each scone lightly with sugar. Bake until the scones are golden, about 18 minutes.

Let the scones cool until warm enough to handle while preparing the filling:

Cherry Cream Cheese Filling:

- 3 oz. cream cheese, softened
- ¼ cup confectioners' sugar
- ¼ teaspoon almond flavoring
- ½ cup finely chopped dried cherries

Mix all ingredients together in food processor until smooth. Fill a pastry bag with a medium tip and pipe the filling into the center of each scone. Alternatively, you can split each scone in half, pile the filling on the bottom, and top with the other half.

Wild Dandelion Salad

With Raspberry Vinaigrette

½ cup toasted walnuts
3 slices cooked bacon, broken, not crumbled
4-5 cups chopped new dandelion leaves
1 hardboiled egg, sliced
¼ cup chopped spring onion

Toss dandelion leaves with bacon, onion, and toasted walnuts.   Plate and drizzle raspberry vinaigrette (recipe follows) over each serving. Top each with decorative slices of egg.

Raspberry Vinaigrette

½ cup extra virgin olive oil
2 tablespoons honey
1 tablespoon Dijon mustard
4 tablespoons red wine vinegar
1 teaspoon fresh lemon juice
salt and pepper to taste
½ cup fresh raspberries

Combine all ingredients in blender and blend until emulsified. Makes about 1 1/4 cups.

Cheese Biscuits

2 cups all-purpose flour
2 ½ teaspoons baking powder
½ teaspoon salt
½ cup butter
1 ½ cups shredded cheddar cheese
2/3 cup milk

Preheat the oven to 425. Lightly grease a baking sheet.

In a mixing bowl, combine flour, salt and baking powder. Cut in butter with a pastry cutter until crumbly.
Stir in the cheese and milk. Mix with a fork until the dough comes together and forms a ball.
Turn the dough out onto a lightly floured board and knead 5 - 6 times. Roll the dough out to a 1 inch thickness. Cut with a 2 inch biscuit cutter.

Bake for 12 - 15 minutes or until light golden brown. Brush lightly with melted butter as soon as biscuits are
removed from oven.

Serve warm with butter or an exotic wine jam like cherry or pinot noir.

Easter Dinner

The Easter table was spectacular. The wine stain had been removed from the white damask tablecloth through some miracle of baking soda and lemon juice. A three-tiered silver candelabra bearing a dozen snow white candles sent sparks of light dancing across every glass, plate, spoon and mirror in the room, and gave off enough heat that everyone was grateful for the breeze that billowed the lace curtains at the open window.   The ham, beautifully browned and glistening with honey glaze, rested on a bed of fresh parsley and red spiced apple rings, and was surrounded— in homage to a tradition only Ida Mae understood and would not deign to explain— by bright yellow deviled eggs sprinkled with paprika. Bowls of garden fresh peas and carrots, roasted new potatoes, and fluffy sweet potato casserole flanked the ham platter, accompanied by buttered corn from last year's garden, a pineapple-cheese casserole that was Ida Mae's specialty, and a basket of fragrant homemade rolls. The table was set with Cici's Havilland china and Bridget's Baccarat crystal   and starched white linen napkins. At each place setting was a bright yellow daffodil in a silver bud vase, courtesy of Lindsay, who collected bud vases.

Having the preacher to dinner was not something that happened every day.

--At Home on Ladybug Farm

Easter Ham

- 1 (8 to 10-pound) smoked ham, bone-in, skin on
- Kosher salt and freshly ground black pepper
- 1 cup (2 sticks) unsalted butter, cut in chunks
- 1 cup orange juice
- ½ cup bourbon
- 1 cup honey
- 1 cup water
- 1/4 teaspoon whole cloves

Preheat the oven to 300 degrees F.

Put the ham in a large roasting pan, fat-side up. Using a sharp knife, score the ham with cuts across the skin, about 2-inches apart and 1/2-inch deep. Cut diagonally down the slashes to form a diamond pattern; season the meat generously with salt and pepper. Place ham in oven.

Melt together in a small saucepan over medium heat the butter, orange juice, honey, water, bourbon and cloves. Slowly cook the liquid down to a syrupy glaze; this should take about 30 to 40 minutes.

Bake ham for two hours; remove and pour glaze over it. Return to oven and continue to bake for 2 hours, basting with the juices every 30 minutes.

Deviled Eggs

6 hard-cooked eggs, peeled and cut lengthwise
¼ cup mayonnaise
½ teaspoon Dijon mustard
1/8 teaspoon salt
¼ teaspoon ground black pepper
Paprika for garnish

Pop out the egg yolks to a small bowl and mash with a fork. Add mayonnaise, mustard powder, vinegar, salt and pepper and mix thoroughly. Fill the empty egg white shells with the mixture and sprinkle lightly with paprika.

Pineapple Cheese Casserole

- 2 (15 ounce) cans pineapple chunks, drained
- 1 cup white sugar
- 1 cup all-purpose flour
- 2 ½ cups shredded sharp Cheddar cheese
- 25 buttery round crackers, crumbled
- ½ cup melted butter

Preheat oven to 350 degrees

Place pineapple in the bottom of a buttered 2 quart casserole dish.

In a small bowl, stir together the sugar, flour and cheese. Add to casserole dish.

Sprinkle crackers over the top of pineapple and cheese mixture. Pour melted butter over the top and bake for 30 minutes.

Sweet Potato Casserole

- 3 cups baked, mashed sweet potatoes
- 1 cup brown sugar
- 2 eggs, lightly beaten
- 1 teaspoon vanilla
- ½ cup heavy cream
- ½ cup melted butter

Mix ingredients with a hand mixer just until combined. Pour into well-buttered 2 quart casserole dish. Add topping (below)

Topping:

- ½ cup brown sugar
- 1/3 cup flour
- 1/3 cup melted butter
- 1 cup chopped pecans

Mix together with fork until crumbly and sprinkle over the top of the sweet potatoes. Bake at 350° for 30 to 40 minutes, until hot and browned.

Ida Mae says...

Bake your sweet potatoes at 400 degrees for one hour. Baking brings out the sweetness.

Summer

Blueberry Season

Blueberry season on Ladybug Farm is heralded by warm bright days, cool nights, and the rows of waxy-leaved bushes whose fruit turns gradually from pale green to pink to frosty blue. The ladies know they will have to fight the birds—and the bugs, and the bees-- for every last berry, but effort is worth it.

Bridget freezes as many berries as she can for use later in the year in muffins and scones.

Ida Mae's Blueberry Scones

Ida Mae says...*Everybody knows scones ain't nothing but biscuits with fruit baked in. Nobody but foreigners makes them in triangles.*

- 1 cup flour
- 1/3 cup sugar
- ½ teaspoon salt
- ¼ teaspoon soda
- 1 egg
- ¼ cup buttermilk
- 2 tablespoons butter
- 1 cup blueberries

Preheat oven to 425

Sift dry ingredients together. Chop the butter into small pieces and mix into the dry ingredients with your fingers or with a pastry cutter until the mixture forms fine crumbs.

Beat the egg. Add buttermilk to the egg mixture and beat to mix.

Mix the wet ingredients into the dry with your hands or with a spoon.

Stir in one cup blueberries, crushing a few with the back of the spoon to release the juices.

Generously butter an 8-inch baking sheet. Ida Mae uses a black iron skillet for hers, but any baking pan will do. Drop mixture by large spoonfuls onto the pan and bake at 425 for 18-20 minutes, until tops are golden brown. About three minutes before the scones are done, brush the tops with buttermilk and sprinkle with two tablespoons of sugar for a nice glaze.

Bridget's Elegant Blueberry Scones

Bridget says...*This makes a very dense, more cake-like scone. The bright taste of lemon-zest is what gives this recipe its zing.*

- 1 ½ cup flour
- ½ cup sugar
- 1/4 teaspoon salt
- 1 ½ teaspoon baking powder
- 1/4 cup butter
- 1 egg
- ½ cup milk
- zest of one lemon, very finely grated
- 1 cup blueberries

Preheat oven to 400.

Stir together first four ingredients. Cut in butter. Add milk and mix until smooth. Toss the blueberries with flour to coat (this keeps them from sinking to the bottom of the pan). Add blueberries to batter. Stir in grated lemon zest.

Generously butter an 8-inch cake pan or scone pan. Pour in the batter. Bake at 400 20-25 minutes, until golden on top and a wooden pick inserted in the center comes out clean.   Cut into narrow wedges and serve hot with butter or lemon curd.

Blueberry Muffins

- 1 cup sugar
- ½ cup butter, softened
- 2 eggs
- ½ teaspoon vanilla extract
- 2 teaspoons baking powder
- 2 ¼ cups flour, divided
- ½ teaspoon salt
- 1 ½ cups blueberries

Preheat oven to 375. Butter 18 muffin cups or use paper liners.

Beat butter, sugar, eggs and vanilla together until smooth. Add baking powder, 2 cups of the flour, and the salt. Beat until smooth.

Toss blueberries with ¼ cup flour. Discard excess flour and gently stir blueberries into batter.

Fill muffin cups 2/3 full. Bake at 375 20-25 minutes.

Bridget says.... *Most people use oil in their muffin recipes. It's the butter that makes these muffins so irresistible!*

Tomato Season

As every gardener knows, there's nothing better than the taste of a fresh tomato, still warm from the vine. You wait all season for the tomatoes to ripen, but when they do, they're all ready at once!

After you've eaten your fill and given away all the tomatoes your neighbors will take, what do you do with the remaining bushels? Here are a few ideas from the ladies of Ladybug Farm.

Tomato Basil Soup

- 1 clove garlic
- 2 tablespoons olive oil
- 6 cups roma tomatoes, peeled, seeded, and cut up
- ½ cup lightly packed fresh basil
- 1 tablespoon sugar
- ¼ teaspoon salt
- 1 cup beef broth
- Dash red pepper

Saute garlic in olive oil until tender. Add remaining ingredients. Bring to boiling, then reduce heat. Cover and simmer for 30 minutes. Transfer to blender (working in small batches) and process until smooth. Garnish with fresh basil . May be served hot or cold.

Tomato Soup with Caramelized Onions

3 large onions, peeled and sliced
1 stick butter
10-12 large garden tomatoes , peeled and chopped
2 tablespoons sugar
3 cups beef broth
1 cup red wine
Salt to taste

Melt butter in a large, heavy pan over medium heat. Add onions. Cook, stirring frequently, until onions are wilted and caramel in color, about 30 minutes.

In a large stock pot add tomatoes, broth, and caramelized onions. Cover and simmer over low heat approximately one hour. Add sugar and wine and continue to cook ½ hour more. Taste and add salt if necessary.

Use an immersion blender to break up onions and tomatoes, but do not puree.

Serve hot, or freeze in quart containers for a winter's day.

Ida Mae says....
The easiest way to peel tomatoes is to drop them into a pot of boiling water until the skins crack. Immediately place them in ice water until cool enough to handle. The skins slide right off!

Fresh Tomato Soup

- 4 cups peeled, chopped fresh tomatoes
- 1 sliced onion
- 2 cups chicken broth
- 2 tablespoons butter
- 2 tablespoons all-purpose flour
- 1 teaspoon salt
- 2 teaspoons sugar

Sautee onion in 2 tablespoons butter until tender. Add flour and stir quickly until thickened. Add chicken broth, a little at a time, stirring to avoid lumps. Add tomatoes, salt and sugar and simmer, covered, for 30 minutes. Transfer to a blender and blend until smooth.

Cream of Tomato Soup

- 6 large garden tomatoes, peeled and chopped
- 1 small onion, diced
- ½ stick butter
- 1 ½ cups chicken broth
- ½ cup heavy cream
- ½ teaspoon salt, or to taste

In a heavy 4 quart sauce pan, sauté onion in butter until translucent. Add chicken broth, tomatoes and salt. Simmer, covered, thirty minutes.

Transfer soup to a blender in batches, or use an immersion blender, and blend until smooth.   Return to pan and stir in cream. Cook to warm, but do not boil.

 Serve warm or cold with a dollop of sour cream and crusty croutons.

Tomato Okra Soup

- 2 tablespoons butter
- 1 small onion, diced
- 1 small clove garlic, minced
- 1 rib celery, sliced
- 2 cups chicken broth
- 4 large tomatoes, peeled and roughly chopped
- 4 cups sliced fresh okra
- 1 cup cooked (or canned) corn
- 1 teaspoon Cajun seasoning
- dash freshly ground black pepper
- salt, to taste

In a medium saucepan, melt butter over medium-low heat. Add onion, garlic, and celery; cook and stir until celery is tender. Add chicken broth, tomatoes, sliced okra, corn , Cajun seasoning, and pepper. Bring to a boil. Reduce heat to medium-low, cover, and simmer for 30 minutes, or until okra is tender. Add salt to taste.

Tomato Chowder

- 4 bacon strips, cooked and crumbled
- 1/4 cup butter or margarine
- 1/4 cup all-purpose flour
- 2 cups chicken broth
- 2 fresh tomatoes, peeled and diced
- 2/3 cup half-and-half cream

Melt butter in a medium saucepan. Stir in flour until smooth. Gradually whisk in broth. Bring to a boil; cook and stir for 2 minutes or until thickened. Stir in tomatoes; heat through. Reduce heat; stir in cream. Heat through (do not boil). Stir in bacon and serve.

Bridget says...

Make sure you cook your bacon fresh for this recipe. Don't use packaged pre-cooked bacon.

Company's Coming

Nothing is more exciting for the ladies of Ladybug Farm than having company. Whether they are entertaining overnight guests, or a group of friends for lunch, the floors are polished, the windows are gleaming, the linens are starched and the table is set with all their best. Ida Mae has even been known to iron the dishtowels!

Bridget brings out her richest desserts, Ida Mae makes sticky buns, and there's always plenty of breakfast casserole. As the day draws to a close, guests are invited to pull up a chair on the porch, pour a glass of wine, and enjoy one of the Shenandoah Valley's spectacular sunsets. Because one thing is certain: when you come visiting at Ladybug Farm, you're family.

Breakfast Casserole

- 6 slices day-old bread
- 1 lb mild sausage, cooked and drained
- 2 cups shredded cheddar cheese
- 6 eggs, beaten
- 2 cups milk
- 1 teaspoon dry mustard
- ½ teaspoon salt

Preheat oven to 350

Grease the bottom of a 9"x13" pan. Tear bread into one-inch chunks. Sprinkle cooked crumbled sausage over bread pieces. Sprinkle cheddar cheese over the sausage. Mix eggs, milk, salt and mustard together; pour over casserole. Bake at 350° for 35 to 40 minutes.
Serves 4 to 6.

Bridget's Amaretto Peach Cobbler

Preheat oven to 400

- 6 fresh sweet peaches, peeled and sliced
- ¼ cup sugar
- 2 tablespoons amaretto

For Topping

- 1 stick very soft butter
- 1 cup sugar
- 1 cup flour
- 1 tablespoon amaretto
- ¼ tsp salt
- ¼ cup milk

Preheat oven to 400
Butter an 8-9 inch oven proof glass casserole dish.
Toss the peaches with ¼ cup sugar and 2 tablespoons amaretto and set aside
Mix butter, sugar, flour, 1 tablespoon amaretto, salt, and milk until smooth.
Pour peach mixture into buttered casserole dish. Top with batter. Bake in 400 degree oven for 20-30 minutes until golden and bubbly.

Serve warm with vanilla ice cream.

Beaten Biscuits

- 2 cups flour
- 1/4 teaspoon salt
- 1/4 teaspoon baking powder
- 2 tablespoons sugar
- 1/4 cup chilled butter cut into small pieces
- 1/3 cup light cream
- water if needed

Preheat oven to 450.
Sift flour, salt, baking powder and sugar together.
Cut in the butter with your hands or a pastry cutter until mixture looks like coarse meal
Use a standing mixer on low to mix dough. Add cream slowly until dough forms a ball. Add water if too dry.
Turn out onto a marble slab or floured wooden board and knead slightly.
With a mallet beat the dough into a rectangle.
Fold dough over then beat it out again.
Repeat this process until the dough becomes white and blisters form (about 15 minutes).
Roll out dough to 1/4" thick.
Cut into 2 inch rounds and prick top with the tines of a fork.
Place on greased baking sheets and bake for 15 minutes

Bridget says...
Now that we have therapists to help deal with our frustrations, no one makes beaten biscuits anymore. But at least you don't have to worry about the calories—you use them all making the biscuits!

A Formal Luncheon

They were ready.

Four glasses of chilled peanut soup were lined up on the top shelf of the refrigerator. Maryland crab cakes and honey-glazed fried chicken were ready to be dropped into separate pans for frying, with the dill caper butter softening near the stove. The mini-quiches and caramelized onion tarts were baking, and the brie en croute was ready to be popped into the second oven. The midori sauce just needed to be heated. A bowl of chopped fresh heritage tomatoes, perfectly seasoned with herbs that had been cut from the garden only that morning, was ready to be spread on crisp garlic- infused baguette slices and topped with goat cheese. And, even though it was not part of the menu, Bridget had made a double fudge cake to be served with her special caramel sauce and fresh lavender whipped cream.

The porch was decorated with four round tables covered in multicolored calico topped with Battenberg lace. All four tables displayed centerpieces of roses fresh from their garden in various heirloom containers- a silver teapot, a china bowl, a coffee urn- and set with an eclectic mix of Limoges and Havilland. White Irish linen napkins trimmed with hand tatting were rolled inside twig napkin rings, each one accented with a rose bud. Even though it was two o'clock in the afternoon, candles flickered in crystal water glasses, and the flames were reflected in the cut glass wine glasses at each place setting.   Only one table had chairs around it, and on that table was a tray of four sparkling mimosas in champagne flutes.

Lindsay and Bridget looked cool and collected in light summer dresses, with their hair swept back and their makeup touched up at least twice in the past hour. Rebel was in the barn with a padlock on the door. The gate to the chicken yard, likewise, was latched and locked. The goat and the deer were in separate stalls inside the barn. And the smell of fertilizer was, for the most part, but a distant memory.   They were ready.

--Love Letters from Ladybug Farm

Peanut Soup

- 2 cups chicken stock
- 2 tablespoons chopped onion
- 1 tablespoon butter
- ½ cup peanut butter
- ½ cup milk
- Chopped peanuts for garnish

Sauté the onions in butter until tender. Add chicken stock and simmer for 10-20 minutes. Add peanut butter and stir until melted. Do not boil. Transfer mixture to blender (or use an immersion blender) and process until blended. Return to heat and add milk. Simmer until warmed through, but do not boil.

May be served hot, or delicious cold, served in martini glasses with cheese straws. Garnish with chopped peanuts before serving.

Honey-Glazed Fried Chicken

2 pounds boneless skinless chicken breasts, cut into 2-inch pieces
1 egg, beaten
¼ cup milk
½ cup flour
½ teaspoon salt
1/8 teaspoon pepper
Vegetable oil for frying

Glaze:

1/3 cup butter
1/3 cup honey
1 teaspoon cinnamon
½ cup finely ground pecans

Mix together flour, salt and pepper. In a separate bowl, beat eggs and milk until combined. Dip chicken pieces in egg mixture, then in flour mixture. Heat 1/2 inch oil in a large frying pan over medium high heat and add chicken in batches. Do not over-crowd. Cook until chicken golden brown, turning as needed. Drain on paper towels, and keep warm while preparing the glaze.

Melt butter in a small saucepan and add honey and cinnamon, stirring until honey is melted. Immediately dip pieces of warm chicken in the glaze and roll in crushed pecans.

Mini Quiches

1 cup grated Cheddar
3 tablespoons flour
3 eggs, beaten
2/3 c. mayonnaise
1 cup broccoli, fresh or frozen, chopped very fine
8 slices bacon, cooked, crumbled
½ cup fresh mushrooms, chopped
½ teaspoon salt
Dash of freshly ground pepper

Preheat oven to 350. Grease 24 mini muffin cups.

In a medium bowl stir flour into cheese.. Add remaining ingredients; mix well. Fill muffin cups with mixture. Bake at 350 degrees for 20 minutes or until set. Let cool slightly before removing from tins.

Caramelized Onion Tart

- 6 medium sized sweet onions, like Vidalia, sliced
- 1 stick butter
- 3 eggs
- ½ cup heavy cream
- ¼ teaspoon nutmeg
- 1 teaspoon salt
- 3 slices Swiss cheese
- 1 tablespoon prepared Dijon mustard
- 1 9 inch pie crust

Preheat oven to 350
Melt butter in a large, heavy skillet. Add onions and cook over medium heat, stirring occasionally, until onions are soft and browned, forming a thick caramel colored sauce.

Beat together eggs, cream, nutmeg, and salt.

Brush the bottom of the pie crust with mustard. Place caramelized onions in the crust and top with cheese. Pour the egg mixture on top.

Bake at 350 for 30-35 minutes, until top is golden brown.

Wedding Dinner Menu

***Appetizer*:** Three berry fruit cup in balsamic vinaigrette topped with gorgonzola crumbles and toasted black walnuts, served with miniature cheese biscuits

***Soup*:** Chilled cantaloupe soup with mint and crème fraiche

***Entree*:** Free range roast turkey wrapped in applewood smoked bacon served on a bed of fresh cherry conserve and accompanied by fingerling potatoes and baby carrots sautéed in rosemary-infused olive oil

Summer squash soufflé

Garden fresh green beans , lightly sautéed and tossed with thyme, toasted almonds and baby onions

***Dessert*:** Strawberry crumble topped with homemade vanilla ice cream

--Love Letters From Ladybug Farm

Three Berry Fruit Cup

- ½ cup extra virgin olive oil
- ½ cup white balsamic vinegar
- 1 clove crushed garlic
- 2 tablespoons fresh minced thyme
- 1 tablespoon fresh chopped mint
- 1 pinch salt
- ground black pepper to taste
- 1 cup blackberries
- 1 cup blueberries
- 1 cup raspberries
- Gorgonzola cheese for garnish
- ½ cup black walnuts, chopped and toasted, for garnish

In a small bowl, whisk together olive oil, white balsamic vinegar, garlic, and mustard powder. Season to taste with salt and black pepper.

Combine berries in a large bowl. Toss lightly with vinaigrette

Serve in individual bowls or glasses. Top each with one tablespoon crumbled gorgonzola cheese and one tablespoon toasted black walnuts

Chilled Cantaloupe Soup
with mint and crème fraiche

- 1 cantaloupe - peeled, seeded and cubed
- 2 cups orange juice
- 1 tablespoon fresh lemon juice
- 1/4 cup fresh mint

1. Peel, seed, and cube the cantaloupe.
2. Place cantaloupe, 1/2 cup orange juice and mint in a blender or food processor; cover, and process until smooth. Transfer to large bowl. Stir in lemon juice and remaining orange juice. Cover, and refrigerate for at least one hour. Garnish with mint and crème fraiche (recipe follows)

Crème Fraiche:

1 cup heavy whipping cream
1 tablespoon buttermilk

In a medium saucepan over low heat, warm the cream to 105 degrees F. Remove from heat and stir in the buttermilk. Transfer the cream to a large bowl and allow this mixture to stand in a warm place, loosely covered with plastic wrap, until thickened but still of pouring consistency. Stir and taste every 6 - 8 hours. This process takes anywhere from 24 to 36 hours, depending on your room temperature. The crème fraiche is ready when it is thick with a slightly nutty sour taste. Chill cream, in the refrigerator, for several hours.

Roasted Turkey In Applewood Bacon

- 1 fresh, not frozen, free range turkey, approx. 15 lbs.
- Juice of a lemon
- Salt and pepper
- ½ cup butter
- 1 yellow onion, peeled and quartered
- Tops and bottoms of a bunch of celery
- 2 carrots
- Parsley
- Sprigs of fresh rosemary
- 6 -8 slices applewood-smoked bacon
- 2 cloves garlic, halved

24 hours in advance:

Brine the turkey overnight by placing it in a mixture of 1 cup salt to one gallon water (or water to cover) and refrigerate, covered, for 6-12 hours.

In the morning, remove the turkey from the brine and discard the brine. Wash the turkey with water and pat dry.

Preheat the oven to 400 degrees F.

Lather the inside of the cavity with the juice of half a lemon. Take a small handful of salt and rub all over the inside of the turkey. Quarter the lemon and place inside the cavity of the turkey.

Add the onion, peeled and quartered, a bunch of parsley, a couple of carrots, and some tops and bottoms of celery.

Make small slits beneath the skin and insert the quartered garlic and sprigs of rosemary. Wrap the turkey in applewood smoked bacon and secure with metal skewers. Make sure that the turkey's legs are tied together, held close to the body, and tie a string around the turkey body to hold the wings in close.

Place turkey BREAST DOWN on the bottom of a rack over a sturdy roasting pan big enough to catch all the drippings

Cook at at **400** F for the **first 1/2 hour**. Then reduce the heat to **350** F for the **next 2 hours**. Then reduce the heat further to **225** F for the next hour to **hour and a half**.

Turn the turkey over for **the last 15 minutes** of cooking, at an oven temp of **300**°F, to brown the breast.

Turkey is done when a meat thermometer inserted into the thigh reads **175**. Let turkey rest out of the oven for 15-20 minutes, and carve breast side up.

Serve on a bed of cherry conserve (recipe follows)

Cherry Conserve

- 2 pounds sweet cherries, pitted

- 1 orange

- 4 cups sugar

- Juice of 1/2 lemon

- 1 cup seedless raisins

- 1 cup chopped pecans

Chop the cherries coarsely .
Seed the orange and slice very thin.
Mix the cherries, sliced orange, sugar, and lemon juice in a large
pan; cook slowly, stirring, until the mixture is thick and
transparent. Add the raisins and nuts and continue cooking 5
minutes.

Summer Squash Soufflé

- 2 pounds sliced yellow summer squash
- 1 medium onion, chopped
- 1 teaspoon salt
- 1 cup milk
- 2 eggs, lightly beaten
- 3 tablespoons melted butter
- 3 tablespoons flour
- 1 cup shredded cheddar cheese
- seasoned salt and pepper, to taste
- buttered bread crumbs

Combine squash, onion, and salt in a large saucepan; cover with water and simmer until vegetables are tender, about 15 to 20 minutes. Drain and mash well. Stir in milk, eggs, melted butter, flour and cheese. Add salt and pepper to taste. Preheat oven to 350°. Bake in a buttered 1 1/2-quart casserole for about 30 minutes. Top with buttered bread crumbs and bake for about 10 minutes longer.

Bridget says...
Technically, this is more of a casserole than a soufflé, but it's so light and airy no one minds if I call it a soufflé!

Strawberry Crumble

- 2 cups sliced strawberries
- ½ cup sugar
- 2 cups flour
- 4 teaspoons baking powder
- 1 cup sugar
- 1 teaspoon salt
- ½ cup butter
- 2/3 cup milk
- 1 egg, slightly beaten
  ### *TOPPING:*
- ¼ cup butter
- ¼ cup sugar
- ½ cup flour

Cover strawberries with ½ cup sugar and set aside. Sift flour, baking powder, 1 cup sugar, and salt. Cut in butter. Combine milk with egg and stir into flour mixture, blending well. Pour strawberry-sugar mixture into well-buttered baking dish, top with batter. Mix together ¼ cup butter, ¼ cup sugar and ½ cup flour with a fork. Sprinkle over mixture in baking pan. Bake at 350 until bubbly and golden brown, 20-30 minutes. Serve with homemade vanilla ice cream (recipe follows)

Homemade Vanilla Ice Cream

4 egg yolks
1/2 pint whole milk
1/2 pint heavy cream
1 cup sugar
1 vanilla pod (scored down the middle)
1 tablespoon vanilla extract

Pour the milk into a saucepan and bring slowly up to boiling point but do not boil. Remove from heat and place the vanilla pod into the mixture. Leave to infuse for about 20 minutes.

In a bowl, beat and mix together the egg yolks and sugar until thick. Carefully remove the vanilla pod from the pan of milk and scrape out the seeds into the milk. Pour the milk into the mixture of egg yolks and sugar while stirring. Pour the mixture back into the pan and heat gently, stirring until the custard thickens , but do not boil. Remove from heat and stir in vanilla extract. Cool in refrigerator 6 hours or overnight. Stir the cream into the cold custard base and transfer the whole mixture into an ice cream maker. Freeze according to manufacturer's directions.

Harvest Time

They made zucchini bread, zucchini casserole, fried, sautéed and roasted zucchini. They made squash soup, tomato soup, onion soup and enough marinara sauce to open an Italian restaurant. They chopped pears for chutney and simmered them into a sweet thick sauce and ate them whole, with juices dripping down their wrists and chins, over the sink. Everything else was put on hold for a season that wouldn't wait, and the abundance of nature's harvest took over their lives.

They bought a second freezer and installed it in the cellar. They shaved corn off the cob and packed it into plastic pint containers, blanched green beans, lima beans, okra and field peas and did the same. And of course they couldn't ignore the bounty of their own fruit trees and bushes when they began to produce. Bridget added twenty-seven glistening jars of blackberry jam to the raspberry coulis in the pantry, and at least as many jars of cherry jelly, grape jelly and apple sauce.   They wondered out loud just how long gardens could possibly continue to produce in this region, anyway.

--A Year on Ladybug Farm

Zucchini Casserole

- 3 large, unpeeled zucchini, sliced
- ¼ cup chopped onion
- 1 (10.75 ounce) can condensed cream of chicken soup
- 2 cups shredded cheddar cheese
- 1 cup sour cream
- 1 stick unsalted butter, melted
- 3 cups dry bread crumbs
- ½ teaspoon salt
- ¼ teaspoon black pepper

Preheat oven to 350 degrees.

Butter a 9x13 inch baking dish.

Boil the zucchini and onion in water for 5 minutes; drain well. In a medium bowl, combine the soup, sour cream and cheese. Stir in the zucchini and onion and mix well.

In a separate medium bowl, combine the butter, bread crumbs, salt and pepper. Spread half of this mixture into the bottom of a 9x13-inch baking dish. Spoon the zucchini mixture over the bread crumbs, then top off with the other half of the bread crumb mixture.

Bake at 350 degrees for 25 to 30 minutes, or until golden brown.

Zucchini Bread

3 eggs
1 cup vegetable oil
1 ¾ cups sugar
2 cups grated zucchini
1 teaspoon vanilla
3 cups flour
½ teaspoon salt
½ teaspoon baking powder
1 teaspoon baking soda
1 teaspoon nutmeg
1 tablespoon cinnamon
½ cup pecans

Preheat oven to 350. Grease and flour two loaf pans.

 Mix together eggs, oil, sugar, zucchini, and vanilla with electric mixer until smooth. Add remaining ingredients and mix until well combined.

 Pour into 2 greased and floured loaf pans. Bake at 350° for approximately 45 to 50 minutes or until the center springs back when touched.

Butternut Squash Soup

- 1 medium (3 pound) butternut squash
- 2 tablespoons butter
- 2 tablespoons brown sugar
- 1 teaspoon nutmeg
- 1 medium onion, halved
- 6 cups chicken stock
- Salt and freshly ground black pepper
- ½ cup heavy cream
- Sour cream for garnish

Preheat oven to 400.

Cut squash in half and scoop out seeds and stringy flesh. Place squash, cut side up, on an oiled baking sheet. Fill the hollow of each half of the squash with 1 tablespoon butter, 1 tablespoon brown sugar, and ½ teaspoon nutmeg. Top with halved onion.

Roast squash and onion mixture 30-45 minutes until squash is very soft. Remove from oven and set aside until cool enough to handle.

Scoop all of the squash flesh and the onion into a saucepan. Be sure to include any juices or spices that remain on the baking sheet. Add chicken stock and simmer 30 minutes to blend flavors. Transfer to a blender and blend until smooth. Return to saucepan, add salt and pepper to taste, and stir in cream. Heat through . Serve warm with a dollop of sour cream.

Harvest Marinara Sauce

- 12 medium ripe tomatoes, peeled and chopped
- 2 large onions, peeled and diced
- 6 cloves garlic, peeled and minced
- ¼ cup olive oil
- 1 green bell pepper, chopped
- 2 carrots, chopped
- ¼ cup fresh basil, chopped
- ¼ cup fresh oregano, chopped
- ¼ c fresh marjoram or thyme, chopped
- 1 cup Burgundy wine
- 1 bay leaf
- 2 stalks celery
- 2 tablespoons tomato paste
- 2 tablespoons beef bouillon granules

In a large soup pot, heat olive oil on medium heat. Add onions and cook until caramelized. Add the garlic and fresh herbs and cook for 5 minutes. Do not allow garlic to brown. Add remaining ingredients and cook on low, covered, stirring occasionally for about 2 hours. Working in batches, transfer all but 1 cup of the sauce to a blender and blend until smooth. Add 1 cup of unprocessed sauce for texture, and stir to mix well. Salt and pepper to taste.

Miss Emily's Cook Book

"I love Brunswick stew." Cici leaned in to peer at the recipe. "Tomatoes, butterbeans, onions, corn... this is perfect! We can use all these vegetables in one big stew!"

Bridget wrinkled her nose and she dragged her finger down the list of ingredients. "Venison..."

"Use beef," suggested Cici.

"Duck..."

"Chicken."

"Hog jowls?"

"Pork loin."

"It says here to slow roast the meat on a spit over an open fire."

Now it was Cici's turn to wrinkle her nose. "When was that thing written anyway? During the American Revolution?"

Bridget looked up from the book. "Wait. We've got Lindsay's propane grill stored in the barn. We haven't used it all summer."

"We've been too busy peeling vegetables."

"That's an open flame, isn't it?"

"It sure is," agreed Cici. "We can get rid of every last vegetable in this kitchen today!"

--A Year on Ladybug Farm

Miss Emily's Brunswick Stew
As interpreted by Cici

Rub for meats:
- 4 tablespoons paprika
- 4 tablespoons kosher salt
- ½ cup brown sugar
- 2 tablespoons freshly ground black pepper
- 1/2 tablespoon cayenne pepper
- 2 tablespoon onion powder
- 2 tablespoon garlic powder
- 2 tablespoons olive oil

Mix all ingredients together. Rub on meats.

- 3-4 lb boneless pork loin roast
- 4-5 pound boneless beef chuck roast
- 2-3 pounds skinless boneless chicken thighs and breasts

Prepare barbecue grill to medium high heat. Add 1 cup hickory chips that have been soaked in water for 30 minutes and drained. Immediately place meats that have been prepared with barbecue rub on the grill and close the top of the grill to infuse with flavor. Watch for flame-ups as the fat content of the meat and the sugar in the rub will burn quickly.   The object is to sear the meat, blacken the rub, and infuse with smoke. The meat does not have to be cooked through, although it is helpful if most of the fat is seared off.

Remove meats from grill when outer crust is brown or slightly charred. Let rest until cool enough to handle. Chop meats roughly, removing and discarding any fat.

In a large (5 gallon or larger) stew pot combine

- 1 gallon peeled fresh tomatoes, chopped
- 2 quarts fresh corn
- 2 quarts shelled fresh butterbeans
- 1 quart sliced fresh okra (optional)
- ¼ cup Worcestershire sauce, or more to taste
- ½ cup apple cider vinegar

Add chopped meats to this mixture and bring to a boil. Reduce heat immediately and simmer for 2-3 hours, until all meats are cooked through and vegetables are soft. Taste broth and season if necessary.

Transfer in batches to a food processor, and grind until meats and vegetables are blended. Return all batches to the pot and cook for 20-30 minutes to blend flavors. Taste against for seasoning.

Freeze in quart containers to enjoy all winter!

Bridget's Apple Currant Pie

- ¼ cup bourbon
- 1 cup currants
- 1 ½ cup sugar
- 1 ½ cup flour
- 1 teaspoon cinnamon
- ½ teaspoon nutmeg
- ¼ teaspoon salt
- ¼ teaspoon ground cloves
- 6 peeled and sliced Granny Smith apples
- 2/3 cup firmly packed brown sugar
- ½ cup butter
- 1 10 inch pie crust

In a small bowl, combine bourbon and currants. Cover and let stand overnight.

Preheat oven to 375.

Prepare a 10 in pie crust, or a 9 inch deep dish crust

In a large bowl, mix 1 ½ cups granulated sugar, ½ cup flour, spices, and salt.

Remove currants from bourbon with a slotted spoon; reserve bourbon. Add currants and apples to sugar mixture and mix well.
Pour filling into unbaked 10-inch pie pastry in pan. Drizzle evenly with reserved bourbon

In another bowl, mix 1 cup flour and the brown sugar.
Add butter and cut in with a pastry blender or rub with your
fingers until mixture forms small lumps.
Sprinkle topping evenly over filling.
Set pie on a baking pan and bake at 375 degrees 55 to 65
minutes. Cover loosely with foil if pie crust browns too quickly.
Pie is done when apples are tender and juices bubble to the top.

Comfort Food

There's something about a cold north wind, night that comes too early, and a fire crackling in the fireplace that makes everyone crave creamy, fatty, high-carb dishes... otherwise known as comfort food.

Comfort food is a specialty of mothers everywhere, whether it be served at the kitchen table or wrapped in a care package to a college student or a soldier overseas. As Lori says in ***Love Letters from Ladybug Farm:***

Can you e-mail me some mac and cheese?:)

Three-Cheese Macaroni

- 2 cups cooked pasta—penne, angel hair, elbow macaroni, or a mixture of your favorites
- 2 tablespoons butter
- 1/4 cup flour
- Salt and pepper to taste
- 1/4 teaspoon nutmeg
- 1 cup milk
- 1/4 cup shredded asiago cheese
- 1/4 cup sharp white cheddar, grated
- 1/4 cup shredded Swiss cheese
- 2 cups grated yellow cheddar
- 1/3 cup dry bread crumbs
- 2 tablespoons butter

Melt butter in a two quart saucepan. Add flour, salt, pepper and nutmeg. Stirring continuously, slowly add milk. Add asiago, sharp white cheddar, and Swiss cheeses and cook and stir over low heat until cheeses are melted and mixture starts to thicken. Remove from heat.

In a small buttered casserole dish layer half the pasta. Sprinkle with 1 cup grated yellow cheddar. Pour half the cheese sauce over this. Top with remaining pasta, remaining cheese sauce, and a mixture of 1 cup cheddar and 1/3 cup bread crumbs. Dot with butter.

Bake at 350 until bubbly and golden brown, approximately 20 minutes

Buttermilk Cornbread

- 1 cup cornmeal
- 1/3 cup all-purpose flour
- 1/4 teaspoon baking soda
- 1 teaspoon baking powder
- 1 teaspoon salt
- 1 egg, beaten
- 1 cup buttermilk

Heat oven to 400. Slather a 9 inch iron skillet with grease and place inside the oven to heat.

Combine dry ingredients; add beaten egg and buttermilk, mixing well. Pour into greased, heated 9-inch iron skillet. Batter should sizzle and puff up around the edges when it hits the skillet. Bake at 400° for 20 minutes, or until lightly browned.

Ida Mae's Homemade Vegetable Soup

- 1 medium onion, chopped
- 2 tbs. olive oil
- 1 quart (32 oz) peeled chopped tomatoes with juice
- 1 quart (32 oz) butterbeans
- 2 cups corn
- 2 cups peeled, chopped potatoes
- 3 quarts beef stock
- Salt to taste
- 1/3 cup fresh chopped mixed herbs—rosemary, thyme, marjoram, basil or oregano work well
-

In a large stock pan sauté chopped onion in olive oil until tender.   Add remaining ingredients, cover, and simmer on low heat 1-2 hours, until vegetables are tender and flavors are blended. Taste and adjust salt if needed

Note: If freezing, omit potatoes. Cooked potatoes can be added to thawed and reheated soup just before serving, if desired.

Bridget's Beef Stew

- 1/4 cup extra-virgin olive
- 3 tablespoons butter
- 2 cups all-purpose flour
- 2 to 3 pounds cubed beef stew meat
- Sea salt and freshly ground black pepper
- 1 cup Burgundy wine
- 8 fresh thyme sprigs
- 3 garlic cloves, smashed
- 2 bay leaves
- 3 cups beef stock
- 9 small new potatoes, scrubbed clean and cut in half
- 6 carrots, peeled and sliced
- 2 small onions, quartered
- 1 cup garden peas frozen or fresh
- 4 large tomatoes, peeled and quartered, or 2 16 oz. cans tomatoes with juice

Preheat a large heavy-bottomed saucepan or Dutch oven over medium-high heat and melt the oil and butter.

Season the beef with salt and pepper, dredge in flour, and brown all of the cubes in the hot oil mixture on all sides. Add remaining ingredients, cover and cook on low heat for 2 1/2 hours.

Chicken With Cracked Cranberry Dressing

6 lb. hen

DRESSING:

1 stick butter
1 cup finely chopped celery
1 medium onion, minced
½ cup fresh or frozen cranberries
4 squares cornbread, crumbled
4 slices toast, diced
1 teaspoon poultry seasoning
1 egg
½ teaspoon salt
¼ teaspoon pepper
¾ cup chicken broth

2 tablespoons butter for hen

Sauté celery, onion and cranberries in butter until onion is translucent and cranberries are cracked. Mix cornbread and toast with poultry seasoning, salt, pepper and egg. Add vegetable mixture and chicken broth. Mix so all ingredients are moist. Rub hen with one tablespoon butter. Cut remaining tablespoon into small pieces and insert under skin. Stuff the dressing loosely into the neck and body cavities. Roast 2 ½ -3 hours at 325 degrees. Leftover dressing may be baked separately for the last 45 minutes of roasting.

Roast Pork Loin

- 3 cloves garlic, minced
- 3 tablespoons fresh rosemary, plus 10-12 sprigs to line the serving platter
- salt and pepper to taste
- 2 pounds boneless pork loin roast
- 1/4 cup olive oil
- 1/2 cup white wine

Preheat oven to 350 degrees F

Crush garlic with rosemary, salt and pepper, making a paste. Pierce meat with a sharp knife in several places and press the garlic paste into the openings. Rub the meat with the remaining garlic mixture and 1 tablespoon olive oil.

Mix remaining olive oil and wine. Place pork loin in pan and pour the olive oil mixture over it. Cook, turning frequently to baste with pan liquids, until pork is no longer pink in the center, about 2 hours. An instant-read thermometer inserted into the center should read 160 degrees F . Remove roast to a platter lined with rosemary. Serve with pan juices.

Horseradish Mashed Potatoes

- 4 pounds golden creamer potatoes
- Kosher salt and freshly ground black pepper
- 2 cups sour cream
- 1 stick unsalted butter
- 3 tablespoons prepared horseradish
- 2 tablespoons cooking water
- Chopped fresh chives, for garnish

Put the potatoes into a large pot, add 2 tablespoons salt, and cover with cold water. Bring to a boil over medium-high heat and cook until the potatoes are tender, about 20 minutes. Drain the water from the potatoes, reserving 2 tablespoons cooking water. Smash potatoes in a large mixing bowl. Add the sour cream, butter, horseradish and season well with salt and pepper. Garnish with chopped fresh chives. 6-8 servings.

Ida Mae's Bourbon Pecan Pie

- 6 tablespoons unsalted butter, softened
- 1 cup dark brown sugar
- 3 eggs
- 1 teaspoon vanilla extract
- ½ teaspoon salt
- ¾ cup dark corn syrup
- 3 tablespoons bourbon
- 2 cups pecan halves or pieces, divided
- 1 pie shell, 9-inch, unbaked

Beat together the butter and brown sugar until creamy and light. Add eggs, 1 at a time, beating after each addition. Beat in vanilla, salt, corn syrup, and bourbon. Arrange 1 cup pecans on the bottom of the pie shell. Pour pie filling over the pecans, then sprinkle remaining pecans over filling. Bake 55 to 60 minutes at 350° F.

Sticky Buns

- 1 teaspoon white sugar
- 1 package active dry yeast
- 1/2 cup lukewarm water
- 1/2 cup milk
- 1/4 cup white sugar
- 1/4 cup butter
- 1 teaspoon salt
- 2 eggs, beaten
- 4 cups all-purpose flour
- 3/4 cup butter
- 3/4 cup brown sugar
- 1 cup chopped pecans, divided
- 3/4 cup brown sugar
- 1 tablespoon ground cinnamon
- 1/4 cup melted butter

In a small bowl, dissolve 1 teaspoon sugar and yeast in warm water. Let stand until creamy, about 10 minutes. Warm the milk in a small saucepan until it bubbles, then remove from heat. Mix in 1/4 cup sugar, 1/4 cup butter and salt; stir until melted. Let cool until lukewarm.

In a large bowl, combine the yeast mixture, milk mixture, eggs and 1 1/2 cup flour; stir well to combine. Stir in the remaining flour, 1/2 cup at a time, beating well after each addition. When the dough has pulled together, turn it out onto a lightly floured surface and knead until smooth and elastic, about 8 minutes.

Lightly butter a large bowl, place the dough in the bowl and turn to coat with butter. Cover with a damp cloth and let rise in a warm place until doubled in volume, about 1 hour.

While dough is rising, melt 3/4 cup butter in a small saucepan over medium heat. Stir in 3/4 cup brown sugar, whisking until smooth. Pour into greased 9x13 inch baking pan. Sprinkle bottom of pan with 1/2 cup pecans; set aside. Melt remaining butter; set aside. Combine remaining 3/4 cup brown sugar, 1/2 cup pecans, and cinnamon; set aside.

Turn dough out onto a lightly floured surface, roll into an 18x14 inch rectangle. Brush with 2 tablespoons melted butter, leaving 1/2 inch border uncovered; sprinkle with brown sugar cinnamon mixture. Starting at long side, tightly roll up, pinching seam to seal. Brush with remaining 2 tablespoons butter. With serrated knife, cut into 15 pieces; place cut side down, in prepared pan. Cover and let rise for 1 hour or until doubled in volume. Meanwhile, preheat oven to 375 degrees .

Bake in preheated oven for 25 to 30 minutes, until golden brown. Let cool in pan for 3 minutes, then invert onto serving platter. Scrape remaining filling from the pan onto the rolls.

Bridget says...

These are a lot of trouble, but nothing warms a house like the smell of cinnamon and yeast rolls in the morning.

Ida Mae says...

Unless you're the one that's got to get out of bed at four a.m. to make them.

Ida Mae's Meat Loaf

- 2 pounds ground beef
- 1 egg
- 1 onion, chopped
- 2 tablespoons green pepper, chopped
- 1 tablespoon olive oil
- 1 cup milk
- 2 tablespoons Worcestershire sauce
- 1 cup dried bread crumbs
- salt and pepper to taste
- 4 tablespoons brown sugar
- 2 tablespoons prepared mustard
- 2/3 cup ketchup
- ½ cup cheddar cheese

Preheat oven to 350 degrees F

Sauté onion and green pepper in olive oil until tender.

In a large bowl, combine the beef, egg, sautéed vegetables, milk and bread crumbs and Worcestershire. Season with salt and pepper to taste and place in a lightly greased 5x9 inch loaf pan.

In a separate small bowl, combine the brown sugar, mustard and ketchup. Mix well and pour over the meatloaf.

Bake at 350 degrees for 45 minutes. Top with cheddar cheese. Continue cooking for 15 minutes longer.

Christmas

  The annual Huntington Lane Christmas Party, jointly hosted by Cici, Lindsay and Bridget in Cici's home, was an event without parallel. Friends, neighbors, colleagues and families shopped all year for the perfect dress, the just-right shoes, the unprecedented hostess gifts. The ladies themselves held their first organizational meeting in September, and from Labor Day onward the clock was counting down toward what was to be, each and every year, the party that would leave all previous parties in the dust.

  A graceful draped rope of tiny blue lights lined both sides of Cici's driveway from the street to the house. A miniature Christmas tree, decorated in twinkling blue and white lights, adorned the fish pond which was the centerpiece of her front lawn while overhead every branch of every deciduous tree was wrapped in tiny white lights and hung with oversized, interior-lit, blue glass ornaments. The front porch was swaged with greenery and studded with white lights and pink poinsettia leaves, and the double entry doors showcased twin wreaths in which glittery white lights and blue satin ribbon were woven in and out of bouquets of white roses.

  The foyer was dominated by a fourteen foot, snow white Christmas tree done completely in crystal ornaments and blue lights. Every doorway was swaged in fake-snow-frosted greenery that was interwoven with blue satin ribbon and tiny white lights. To the right of the tree was a bar, draped with white satin and decorated with sprays of white roses and a half dozen blue candles, where a bartender made certain every guest was immediately greeted with a cup of creamy Southern Comfort eggnog.   Hidden stereo speakers provided traditional Christmas music as a background to the "Oohs" and "ahhs" and the happy greetings of guests who only saw one another once a year.

In the study, Cici's office furniture had been pushed against the wall and covered by floor-to-ceiling drapes of theatrical scrim which were backlit by red and green up-lights and draped with swags of evergreen tied with elaborate red bows and clusters of sparkly ornaments. In the center of the room was a twelve foot evergreen decorated in gold balls and red and green lights. Surrounding it, Cici had built a circular serving table that was draped in gold lame and lit by dozens of gold candles on mirrors. Behind the table another bartender prepared pomegranate margaritas while guests plucked shrimp from the Christmas-tree shaped tower decorated with red pepper ornaments and filled their gold-colored hors d'oeuvres plates with everything from homemade cheese straws to olives wrapped in prosciutto.

The dining room buffet was an L-shaped spectacle of white satin, silver ornaments and red glass. Rows upon rows of glittering white lights were tucked into nests of greenery and draped through folds of satin, while red glass ball ornaments reflected the sparkle and clusters of red roses accented each serving dish. The Beef Wellington was a work of art with its crispy pastry crust and savory spinach filling, complemented by an asparagus casserole for which Bridget would never reveal the recipe.   The flaky rolls had been three days in the making. Mushrooms had been stuffed and frozen a week in advance. Crispy crab cakes on a heated platter surrounded a silver bowl of remoulade sauce. New potatoes had been tossed with a hot tomato vinaigrette mere moments before serving, and were kept warm with a chafing dish. Vegetarian selections included a broccoli quiche, tomato tarts with black olives, and a six layer cheese,red pepper, and pesto torte.   The desert buffet featured a Christmas tree decorated with sugared fruit and surrounded by a colorful wreath of decorated cookies—all lovingly handmade of course-- bowls of truffles and dipping chocolate, three different layer cakes, and the piece de resistance – individual custard cups, trimmed in silver paper and filled with peppermint cream.

---A Year on Ladybug Farm

Bite Sized Zucchini Tarts

10" × 13" sheet of frozen puff pastry,
thawed and chilled
12 small zucchini (about 2 1/2 lbs.), trimmed
Salt
3 tablespoons butter
1 small onion, finely chopped
10 cherry tomatoes, excess moisture pressed out, finely
chopped
1 cup crumbled feta cheese
½ cup ricotta
2 tablespoons chopped fresh basil
Freshly ground black pepper
1 egg, lightly beaten

. Preheat oven to 350°

Cut rounds of puff pastry to fit 24 well-greased mini muffin
tins. Place pastry in tin and bake about 25 minutes, until
golden. Cool.

Grate 4 zucchini into a large bowl. Add 1 tbsp. of salt, toss
well, and set aside to let weep for 30 minutes. Transfer to
a stack of paper towels and press thoroughly to remove
moisture.

Meanwhile, slice remaining zucchini into 1/4"-thick
rounds. Blanch in a large pot of boiling salted water for 1
minute. Drain and spread out on paper towels.

Heat butter in a large skillet over medium heat. Add
onions and cook until soft, 5–6 minutes. Add grated

zucchini and cook, stirring often, until just beginning to brown, 5–7 minutes. Transfer to a large bowl; let cool.

 Stir tomatoes, egg, half of the feta, ricotta, basil, and salt and pepper to taste into zucchini mixture. Spread mixture evenly in individual crusts. Arrange zucchini rounds, slightly overlapping in rows, like tiles, on top. Bake for 15 minutes, then brush top with reserved butter. Continue to bake until crust is deep golden, 10 minutes more. Let cool to room temperature, then sprinkle remaining feta over top.

Yeast Rolls

- 2 tablespoons butter, softened
- 3 tablespoons white sugar
- 1 cup hot water
- 1 (.25 ounce) package active dry yeast
- 1 egg, beaten
- 1 teaspoon salt
- 2 1/4 cups all-purpose flour
- 1 tablespoon melted butter (for brushing tops of rolls)

Preheat oven to 425 degrees.

In a large bowl, mix the butter, sugar, and hot water. Allow to cool until lukewarm, and mix in the yeast until dissolved. Mix in the egg, salt, and flour. Allow the dough to rise until doubled in size.

Form dough into rolls with your floured hands by pinching off a two-inch section and forming it into a ball. Place rolls on a greased baking sheet, and allow to rise again until doubled in size.

Brush tops of rolls with 1 tablespoon melted butter. Bake for 10 minutes in the preheated oven, or until a knife inserted in the center of a roll comes out clean.

Serve hot with butter and honey.

Beef Wellington

- 6 (4 to 5 ounce) tenderloin steaks
- 1/2 teaspoon salt
- 1/4 teaspoon pepper
- 1/2 cup chopped onion
- 1/3 cup vegetable oil
- 1 cup red wine
- 2 tablespoons brandy
- 1/2 teaspoon fines herbes
- 1 tablespoon butter or margarine, melted
- Spinach Filling (recipe follows)
- Prepared Pastry or Filo dough (from the refrigerated section of your grocer)
- 2 egg yolks
- 2 teaspoons water

Sprinkle steaks with salt and pepper, and place in a shallow dish.

Sauté onion in hot oil until tender.

Add wine, brandy, and herbs.

Pour mixture over steaks; cover and marinate in refrigerator 8 hours.

Drain steaks, reserving marinade.

Sauté steaks in 1 tablespoon butter in a skillet just until lightly browned on both sides.

Place steaks in dish; cover and refrigerate 2 hours.

Meanwhile prepare Spinach stuffing.

Spinach Stuffing:

- 3 tablespoons extra-virgin olive oil
- 1 pound frozen chopped spinach
- 4 cloves garlic, chopped
- 1 to 2 teaspoons red pepper flakes
- 1/2 cup sweet sherry
- 1 cup fresh bread crumbs
- 1/2 cup grated Romano cheese
- Salt and freshly ground black pepper
- 1 teaspoon chopped fresh basil leaves
- 1 teaspoon chopped fresh parsley leaves
- 1 teaspoon chopped fresh chives
- 1 teaspoon chopped fresh rosemary leaves
- 1 teaspoon chopped fresh thyme leaves

Cover and chill at least 2 hours.

Roll pastry into an 18 inch square on a lightly floured surface; cut into six 9 x 6 inch rectangles.
Spread center of each pastry rectangle with 1/3 cup Spinach Filling; top with a steak.
Combine egg yolks and water; brush edges of pastry with mixture.
Fold pastry over, and pinch edges and ends together.
Place Wellingtons, seam side down, on a lightly greased baking sheet.
Brush with egg mixture.
Bake at 400° for 25 minutes or until golden brown.

Combine reserved marinade, beef broth, and tomato paste in a saucepan; cook over medium heat 25 minutes.
Combine cornstarch and Madeira; stir into broth mixture and cook, stirring constantly, until thickened.
Top each Wellington with ¼ cup Madeira sauce to serve.

Chocolate Truffles

- 8 ounces of semi-sweet or bittersweet high quality chocolate, chopped into small pieces
- ½ cup heavy whipping cream

- 1 teaspoon pure vanilla extract
- 2 tablespoons Amaretto
- 1 teaspoon almond extract

- ½-1 cup cocoa powder for coating

In a saucepan over low heat bring the heavy whipping cream to a simmer.

Place the chocolate in a separate bowl. Pour the cream over the chocolate, add the vanilla, Amaretto and almond extract and allow to stand for a few minutes. Stir until smooth. Allow to cool, and place in the refrigerator for two hours.

Remove from refrigerator and with a teaspoon roll out balls of the chocolate mixture. Dust your hands with confectioner's sugar to prevent sticking, and roll between your palms quickly to form balls. Place on a baking sheet lined with parchment paper. Place in the refrigerator overnight.

Roll in cocoa powder and serve.

Makes 30-40 chocolate truffles.

Peppermint Cream

- 1 cup heavy whipping cream
- 3 tablespoons confectioners' sugar
- ½ teaspoon peppermint extract
- 6 hard peppermint candies, crushed

In a chilled small mixing bowl and with chilled beaters, beat cream until it begins to thicken. Add confectioners' sugar and peppermint extract; beat until hard peaks form. Stir in crushed peppermint candies. Red food coloring may be added for a festive touch. Store in the refrigerator.

Maryland Crab Cakes with Remoulade Sauce

- 1 pound fresh lump crabmeat
- 1 ½ tablespoons dry bread crumbs
- 2 teaspoons chopped fresh parsley
- salt and pepper to taste
- 1 egg
- 1 ½ tablespoons mayonnaise
- ½ teaspoon ground dry mustard
- 1 teaspoon Worcestershire sauce
- 2 tablespoons butter

Mix together crabmeat, bread crumbs, parsley, salt and pepper.

Beat together egg, mayonnaise, Worcestershire sauce and mustard. Combine with other ingredients and mix well. Form into six large patties or 12- 18 small ones.

Melt butter in a heavy skillet. Fry crab cakes until a brown crust forms on each side, about four minutes for regular sized cakes.

Serve hot with remoulade sauce (recipe follows).

Remoulade Sauce

- 1 cup mayonnaise
- 2 tablespoons lemon juice
- 1/2 cup chopped onion
- 2 tablespoons chopped garlic
- 2 tablespoons prepared horseradish
- 3 tablespoons prepared whole-grain mustard
- 2 tablespoons Worcestershire sauce
- 3 tablespoons ketchup
- 1 teaspoon salt
- 1/4 teaspoon cayenne pepper
- 1/8 teaspoon freshly ground black pepper

Combine all ingredients in a blender and process until smooth.

Asparagus Casserole

2 tablespoons butter, melted
12 spears fresh asparagus
2 tablespoons onion, diced
¼ cup parmesan cheese
½ cup bread crumbs
½ teaspoon salt
1/8 teaspoon pepper
¼ teaspoon thyme
2 tablespoons sherry

Boil asparagus in boiling water for 3 minutes. Drain well and pat dry.

Pour butter into shallow baking dish. Line bottom with asparagus spears. Mix remaining ingredients together and spread over spears. Cover and bake at 375°F. for 30-35 minutes or until asparagus is tender.

Broccoli Quiche

- 1 9-inch pie shell
- 2 cups chopped fresh broccoli
- I cup thinly sliced fresh mushrooms
- ½ cup milk
- ½ cup heavy cream
- 3 eggs, beaten
- 2 tablespoons butter, melted
- 1 tablespoon flour
- 1 teaspoon salt
- ½ teaspoon pepper
- 1 teaspoon dry mustard
- 1 cup shredded cheddar cheese, divided
- ½ cup asiago grated cheese
- ½ cup mozzarella cheese

Preheat oven to 375 degrees. Bake pie crust about 10 minutes or until bottom is slightly brown. Let cool. Cook broccoli until tender; drain well. Combine milk, eggs, butter, flour, salt, pepper and 3/4 cup cheese; whisk until well blended. Sprinkle remaining 1/4 cup of cheese over crust. Layer broccoli and mushrooms on cheese. Pour milk and egg mixture over all. Bake at 375° for 35 to 45 minutes or until a knife inserted in center comes out clean.

Six Layer Cheese Torte

2 1/2 pounds cream cheese
1/2 pound goat cheese
1 tablespoon roasted garlic
½ cup roasted red pepper pesto
½ cup basil pesto
½ cup sun dried tomato pesto
Toasted pine nuts, for garnish

Directions:

Mix cream cheese, goat cheese, and garlic together. Line a round, greased bowl with plastic wrap. Spray the plastic wrap with non-stick cooking spray. Layer as follows:

1/3 cheese mixture
½ cup red pepper pesto
1/3 cheese mixture
½ cup basil pesto
1/3 cheese mixture
½ cup sun dried tomato pesto

Put in the refrigerator for four hours, then unmold onto a serving platter and remove plastic wrap. Sprinkle with toasted pine nuts for garnish.

Tomato Tarts with Black Olives

- 1 dozen prepared individual tart crusts
- 3 medium tomatoes, peeled
- 3 tablespoons finely chopped thyme
- 6 oz. feta cheese (for a different flavor, you may use ¾ cup shredded sharp cheddar)
- ¾ cup chopped black olives
- 2 tablespoons prepared Dijon mustard

Preheat oven to 350

Slice the tomatoes, sprinkle with salt, a remove moisture by pressing them between a stack of paper towels, and covering them with a heavy object (like an iron skillet) for 30 minutes. Brush the bottoms of each tart with prepared mustard. Dice the tomatoes. Fill each tart halfway full with diced tomatoes, sprinkle with salt and thyme. Crumble cheese on top of tomatoes, top generously with chopped black olives. Bake at 350 20-25 minutes.

Swiss Chard and Goat Cheese Tart

- 1 9 inch pie crust
- 2 tablespoons chopped fresh rosemary
- 1 teaspoon olive oil
- 6 slices bacon
- 2 scallions, chopped
- 1 bunch Swiss chard (leaves only)
- 8 ounces goat cheese

Preheat oven to 350

Rub the pie crust with olive oil and sprinkle with chopped rosemary.

Fry 6 slices of bacon; remove and crumble.

In the bacon fat, sauté scallions and chard leaves until chard is wilted.

Place the chard mixture in the prepared pie crust. Top with crumbled goat cheese. Top with bacon

Bake at 350 for 30 minutes or until bubbly.

Ida Mae's Fruit Cake

- 2 (8 ounce) containers candied cherries
- 1 (8 ounce) container candied mixed citrus peel
- 2 cups raisins
- 1 cup dried currants
- 1 cup dates, pitted and chopped
- 2 (8 ounce) packages pecans
- ½ cup brandy
- 2 ½ cups all-purpose flour
- ½ teaspoon baking soda
- 1 teaspoon ground cloves
- 1 teaspoon ground allspice
- 1 teaspoon ground cinnamon
- ½ teaspoon salt
- 1 cup butter
- 2 cups packed brown sugar
- 6 eggs
- 1 cup molasses
- 1 cup grape juice
- 1 bottle good red wine for marinating

In a medium bowl, combine cherries, citrus peel, raisins, currants, dates, and nuts. Stir in brandy; let stand 2 hours, or overnight. Dredge soaked fruit with 1/2 cup flour.

Preheat oven to 275 degrees F Grease a tube pan fruit cake pan, line with parchment paper, and grease again. In a medium bowl, mix together 2 cups flour, baking soda, cloves, allspice, cinnamon, and salt; set aside.

In a large bowl, cream butter until light. Gradually blend in brown sugar and eggs. Mix together molasses and grape juice. Beat into butter mixture alternately with flour mixture, making 4 dry and 3 liquid additions. Fold in floured fruit. Turn into prepared pan.

Bake in preheated oven for 3 to 3 1/2 hours, or until a toothpick inserted into the center of cake comes out clean. Remove from pan, and lift off paper. Cool cake completely. Pour ½ cup wine over the cake and wrap tightly in a cloth towel, then cover with wax paper.

Pour ½ cup wine over the cake each week until wine is gone, wrapping tightly again after each pouring.

Fruit cake should marinate at least four weeks, and should be started at Thanksgiving to serve by Christmas.

Ladybug Cookies

1 cup butter

1 cup sugar

2 eggs

1 teaspoon peppermint extract

1 ½ cups baking flour

1 teaspoon baking powder

1 teaspoon salt

red food coloring (optional)

Preheat oven to 350.

Mix first four ingredients. Add dry ingredients a little at a time.

Add red food coloring until the dough is a bright red shade.

Cover and refrigerate at least one hour. Roll out 1/4 in thick on floured surface. Cut into circles with a cookie cutter dipped in flour and place on ungreased cookie sheet. Roll one quarter teaspoon of dough into a small ball for each cookie, then flatten and attach the ladybug "head". (This is a great job for children, who can shape the head of each ladybug and give it personality). Bake 8 minutes on ungreased cookie sheet until light golden . Cool and decorate with butter cream frosting (recipe follows) .

Buttercream Frosting

3 cups confectioner's sugar
1 stick butter, softened
2-4 tablespoons milk
1 teaspoon almond flavoring
Red food coloring

Beat softened butter with almond flavoring until fluffy. Add confectioners' sugar, one cup at a time, and beat until smooth. Add milk, one tablespoon at a time, until frosting is of spreading consistency. Add food coloring until a nice shade of red is obtained.

Decorations:

1 bag semi-sweet chocolate chips

Red Decorator's Sugar

Melt ½ bag chocolate chips in a double boiler until smooth. Dip the "heads" of each ladybug into the chocolate and place on wax paper to set.
(cont.)

Frost the body of the ladybug with red buttercream frosting.
While frosting is wet, sprinkle liberally with red sugar (or dip the
cookie in a plate of red sugar and shake off the excess)
Place chocolate chips on the body of the cookie for the
ladybug's spots.

Bridget's Best-Ever Cookies

- 1 cup butter, softened
- ¾ cup packed light brown sugar
- ½ cup white sugar
- 2 eggs
- ½ teaspoon vanilla extract
- ½ teaspoon almond extract
- 2 ½ cups all-purpose flour
- 1 teaspoon baking soda
- ½ teaspoon salt
- ½ cup coarsely chopped pecans
- ¾ cup white chocolate chips
- ½ cup butterscotch chips

Preheat oven to 350 degrees

In a large bowl, cream together the butter, brown sugar, and white sugar until smooth. Beat in the eggs, one at a time, then stir in the vanilla and almond extracts. Combine the flour, baking soda, and salt; gradually stir into the creamed mixture. Stir in the nuts, white chocolate chips and butterscotch chips. Drop dough by teaspoonfuls onto ungreased cookie sheets.

Bake for 10 minutes in the preheated oven, or until golden brown.

Ida Mae's Chocolate Chocolate Chip Cookies

- 1 cup butter, softened
- 1 ½ cups white sugar
- 2 eggs
- 2 teaspoons vanilla extract
- 2 ¼ cups all-purpose flour
- ½ cup cocoa powder
- ¾ teaspoon baking soda
- ¼ teaspoon salt
- 1 cup semisweet chocolate chips
- 1 cup white chocolate chips
- ½ cup chopped walnuts (optional)

Preheat oven to 350 degrees

In large bowl, beat butter, sugar, eggs, and vanilla until light and fluffy. Combine the flour, cocoa, baking soda, and salt; stir into the butter mixture until well blended. Mix in the chocolate chips, white chocolate chips and walnuts. Drop by rounded teaspoonfuls onto ungreased cookie sheets.

Bake for 8 to 10 minutes in the preheated oven, or just until set. Cool slightly on the cookie sheets before transferring to wire racks to cool completely.

Index

Index

Donna Ball is the author of over eighty novels, including A YEAR ON LADYBUG FARM, AT HOME ON LADYBUG FARM and LOVE LETTERS FROM LADYBUG FARM.   She lives in a restored Victorian barn in the heart of the Blue Ridge Divide, where she enjoys entertaining with many of the recipes included in this book.

Made in the USA
Lexington, KY
08 January 2011